BEAVER BOOKS

W9-BIZ-332

My First Bilingual Book · Mon premier livre bilingue

Birthday Party

◆

La fête d'anniversaire

English-French · Français-anglais

— A child's first book of words and fun – in two languages! —
— Un livre bilingue, rempli de mots et de plaisir pour les tout-petits ! —

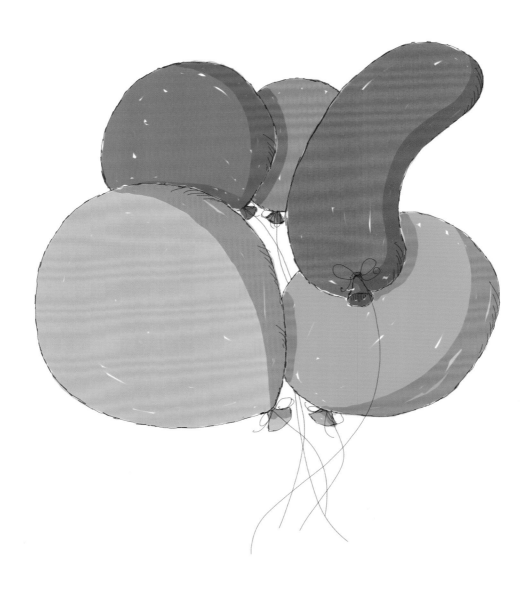

balloons

des ballons

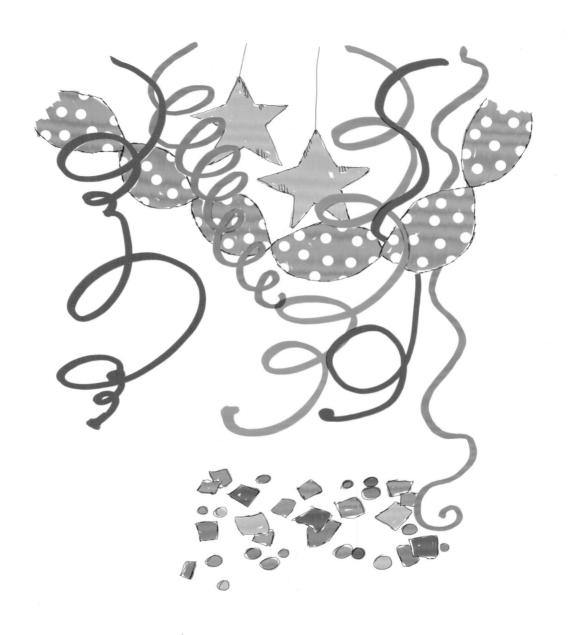

decorations

des décorations

friends

des amis

party hats

des chapeaux de fête

surprise

une surprise

cards

des cartes

gifts

des cadeaux

games

des jeux

noise

du bruit

candles

des bougies

cake

un gâteau

— Fun activities with things at a — birthday party!
— Des activités amusantes! —

Can you say the names of these things at a birthday party, in both French and English?

Nomme en français et en anglais tout ce qui est présenté ici.

Say the name of each thing and find its picture in the book.

Prononce les mots que tu vois ici et retrouve les éléments correspondants dans le livre.

candles　　　**games**　　　**decorations**　　　**noise**
des bougies　**des jeux**　**des décorations**　**du bruit**